Freeing THE
LIGHT WITHIN

A GUIDE TO
THE RADIANCE PRACTICE

CYNTHIA WALKER

CENTRAL FIRE
PRODUCTIONS

ISBN: 978-0-9802354-9-4

LCCN: 2008940379

Cover design by Angela Werneke
RIVER LIGHT MEDIA
awerneke@earthlink.net

Back cover photo: Jennifer Esperanza
www.jenniferesperanza.com

Guatemalan photos © 2008 by Suzanne Eliel, dba Photographer for Life.
www.suzannaeliel@mac.com

Permission to reproduce The Venus Mandala (p. 36) from Walker & Co.,
"The Mayan and Other Ancient Calendars" by Geoff Stray..

Leon Secatero

BEAUTY WAY PRAYER

Si' ah naaghai bik' eh hozhoon
Hozho nahasdlii'
Hozho nahasdlii'
Hozho nahasdlii'
Hozho nahasdlii'

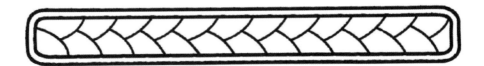

CONTENTS

For All the Teachers
Past • Present • Future

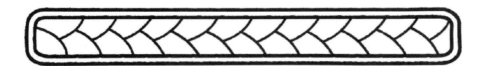

INTRODUCTION

Before I died from my old life and was reborn, it seemed my personal Radiance was something to be hidden, obscured and repressed. My radiance was hidden under a heavy dark robe of my own making. It took many years of weaving it so it appeared "just right" from the outside and did not allow my light to pass through the tightly woven, rough and thorny material. It was hard to weave this cape, the thorns cut me, so my blood also became part of the material of my life. From the outside, the cape had places where other people in my life could put their thoughts, their envy, their expectations, their anger, and I would carry them around with me. The cape became so heavy and dark, it was difficult for me to move with any freedom or lightness; I began to smother under the weight of it all.

In 1987, when I died and went to the other side, I did not want to come back to this life of suffering, but was obedient when the Voice said, "Go back. You're not done yet." When I returned, the cape began to unravel. One day, I asked myself, "Does this still serve me?" I threw the cape down, some of the threads had already begun to rot and decay, it lay there, becoming fertilizer for new growth. I turned, and walked forward on my path, asking for illumination and guidance from the Creator. The Radiance Practice is the Path I took, the natural path to BECOMING. As the mountain is always becoming the plain, we are always becoming who we truly are.

The Radiance practice was gifted to me by my spirit guides in 1995. As I had been asked to hold a workshop in Rhode Island, I prepared myself by asking for guidance in a vision quest. I had recently moved into an old home-

1

stead, built in 1742, with a massive central fireplace made of stone that had been used for cooking in the old days. The oven, for baking bread, was to the side of the great hearth, the heart of the home. A small barn housed my horse, Crystal. Out back were a few acres of tall, yellow grass, dotted with wildflowers, hiding great, granite stones and a spring-fed pool.

I had fasted that day to enhance the reception of the message I knew would come. I settled in on my blanket with my drum, note pad, and an awareness of the natural world all around me. The crows quieted down, the bunnies curled up, the deer rested by the old stone wall at the edge of the field. I could feel the fairies and sense the presence of the little people peeking out at the offering of tobacco I had left for them. Butterflies, bees, and dragonflies paused only for a moment in front of my eyes before carrying on with their business. The wind danced with a shower of apple blossoms, they swirled and twirled before coming to rest at the edge of the garden. Dancing next with the tall pines, the long needles whispered to me before the wind gave me a kiss. The Sun became hotter and more piercing as the day passed. When the rays of the sun were directly overhead, beads of sweat began to form in my hair and drip down my face. I lay down, to see the bears, formed of white clouds, pass by to the west.

Suddenly, in that moment, the steps of the radiance practice unfolded as if a great scroll were being opened before me, the steps were illuminated by pictures of incidents and experiences from my own life. I realized that this practice and the steps of this practice related to my life: it is a metaphor for my life. The struggles, the challenges, the difficulties of childhood, were stepping stones on my spiritual path. My spirit guides showed me the Radiance Practice as a way to heal ourselves through the metaphor of our own personal journeys.

Join me on this path to Radiance. It is our destiny and our time to heal ourselves, to honor and to celebrate who we are as humans. It is time to recalibrate our direction in relationship to the Earth, Air, Water, and the Fire, our Spirit within. This Workbook is designed to retrain our minds, to restore the expansive triumvirate of the body, mind, and spirit for our own healing, and for the healing of all living beings, restoring a state of Grace to our world. This workbook was developed from my journey. Join me as we return to the past and remember the healing times, the adventures, the allies, the initiations. I share with you the hope that on your path you will find your own healing with the guidance offered by the Radiance Practice.

Join me in manifesting a state of GRACE on Earth.

PART I

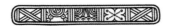

MY JOURNEY
TO RADIANCE

KEME
DEATH,
REINCARNATION,
REBIRTH

DEATH BECOMES ME

According to the Mayan Calendar, 1987 was the year that we passed from the time period known as the Nine Hells to the Thirteen Heavens. I found myself in the gynecologist's office, seeking answers to the cause of the bleeding that was impeding me from road racing, running, biking, tennis, and windsurfing that for so long had been necessary for the sustenance of my well-being.

The blood, my life force, would not stop flowing. I could not maintain the vigorous work schedule of running my own catering business, caring for my home and family, or my social life. I felt weak, exhausted, and as a result of this weakness, unattractive. I felt my husband's attention shift to other, more vitally attractive women.

The gynecologist suggested an exploratory laparoscopy to determine what the problem was. I went to the hospital for the pre-surgical work-up for the lab tests and to meet with the anesthesiologist. He commented on my low pulse rate. I explained that I was very fit and athletic and informed him that from my previous surgical experiences I knew I did not need much to "put me out." He wasn't listening.

Many of our close friends worked at the hospital; it was a major source of stories that kept our party banter full of laugher and jokes, pathos and miracles. Our best friends were a thoracic surgeon, John, and his wife, Sandy. Sandy was also my catering partner, so the two husbands spent a lot of time together while Sandy and I were working in the evenings. I had been listening to the stories from the hospital for too long, and knowing the mischievous

5

nature of John, I gave strict orders for him to "stay away" from the window in my surgical suite during my upcoming procedure.

Groggy, shivering and nauseous when I awoke in the recovery room, I felt something on my right big toe. Struggling to wake up, I asked the nurse "what's on my toe?" She uncovered my foot and was surprised to see an identification tag for the bodies in the morgue. "There's a note here," she said, "It says, 'you're a 10.'" Smiling somewhere inside, I knew John, my friend, had been there for me.

How long it was before they sat me up in a chair I cannot recall. The recovery room was darkened, all the other patients had gone home. A lone nurse was straightening up. The gynecologist and my husband were sitting far from me, with my husband's back to me, I could see the concern on my doctor's face, but I could not hear him. I was angry that he was not explaining directly to me the findings of the exploratory procedure. I would need abdominal surgery to remove three large tumors and my uterus.

Somehow, I recovered from the exploratory surgery just in time to join my family in Rhode Island for the traditional Thanksgiving at the beach. This beach has always felt like my spiritual home, the place I always return to for healing, working things out, crying to and connecting with grandmother ocean, whatever face she is wearing, calm and peaceful, or raging and grasping.

This time, I felt that I had just fallen from the heavens, wondering if it was safe to love here on earth. I felt raw and uncertain. I was facing the prospect of having my uterus removed. I relived the premature birth of my son in 1970, feeling him moving against my legs in the hospital bed while the nurse was trying to push out the afterbirth. My son died a few minutes later. It was seventeen years before I found the place where the hospital buried him; in a corner of the old cemetery in Rhode Island, in a styrofoam box, near other, unnamed babies. There was no marker left when I found the place, I knew it by the great oak that protected the little ones, and by the red tail hawk that flew overhead.

The next year I became pregnant again. Traveling halfway around the world, we moved from Australia, where we had been living for three years I began to miscarry at 7 months. After all preventive measures known at the time were taken, Julia was born. She weighed 2 pounds and 6 ounces. She was in the hospital for three months. They wouldn't let me hold her until she weighed four pounds; it was almost two months from the time of her birth. I recall the featherweight of her in my arms, the overwhelming love, the big blue direct gaze of my precious daughter as we bonded for the first time.

Later, I had an IUD inserted to prevent pregnancy in a painful procedure that caused heavy bleeding. Two years later, when I decided to try pregnancy again, I had developed endometriosis, a side effect of that particular brand of IUD that was later taken off the market and involved in a class action suit.

Six months later, in 1974, I became pregnant again, undergoing a newer method of preventing premature birth that had been developed in India. My cervix was tied with a string to keep it closed for the duration of my pregnancy. I was instructed not to do anything strenuous, not to lift anything, (this included my four year old daughter) This time, I had a difficult delivery; my baby was breech. The baby turned, I was wheeled into the delivery room. I birthed my beautiful daughter, Elizabeth. She was placed in my arms immediately; there was instant recognition and an immediate knowing of one another. She was perfect.

After we were both cleaned up, the nurse brought in my daughter, all wrapped up in her cozy pink blanket. She was wide awake as I took out her hand to admire the wondrous perfection of her nails and the wrinkles of her fingers and wrists. I began to breast feed my baby, something that I was not able to share with my other babies. We sat in peace after our ordeal of birth, nourishing one another in the growing light of the new day. Later that same day I underwent surgery to prevent any more pregnancies. The moment at dawn, nursing my baby, remains, like a joyful golden treasure, locked away in my heart.

As I walked the beach that Thanksgiving, in 1987, the wind behind my back, I could see and understand at a deeper level than ever before, but I didn't know why. Suddenly, my life experiences were illuminated as the tests of life itself. I could see the denial of myself as a powerful and intelligent woman, the denial of the intuitive wisdom of my own body, the sacrifices I had made for others, my early conditioning that I was "less than" simply because I was a female.

No one was listening but the sea, the earth, the wind. In the stark light of my newfound sight I was profoundly comforted by the elements. Turning, the wind now blowing against me, I realized it would take more effort to get "home."

I RECOGNIZE DEATH

The evening before my scheduled surgery, I went to the hospital lab for the meeting with the anesthesiologist. She stood, flipping the papers of my report at the far end of the room. Suddenly, she turned and asked me, "Did you know you died on the operating table?"

Time shifted and tilted as the recognition of my own death brought everything to a standstill in the grey light of the January afternoon.

Memories paralyzed me as if I had lept into cold dark water. Scenes of comprehension floated to the surface: The moment in the recovery room when my husband had his back to me was illuminated with the knowledge that he and the doctor knew I had died, and had kept the information from me. The newfound sight I had acquired enabled me to see into people and gave me a new ability to trust my own instincts.

After the interview with the woman doctor, I went home and confronted my husband. He did not want to talk about it. I made him sit down and listen to me. I explained my last wishes for my children. I felt more at peace after expressing myself and my wishes. There were so many different endings to review and remember; all destined to keep me moving forward on the path of Radiance and into a place of a new beginning, Rebirth.

THE FIRST JOURNEY

I was guided to study Shamanism after a synchronistic meeting with a shaman in Costa Rica where we had taken the family for a two week holiday at Christmas vacation. In 1989, for the second year in a row, we had rented a wonderful house on the Pacific coast of the Nosara Penninsula, lively with howler monkeys, iguanas, sea turtles, and scorpions.

The vegetable bins in the small general store were empty; the truck, filled to capacity with the Christmas delivery, had broken down on the road, leaving us waiting in the garden at the back of the store under the shady branches of a tree filled with chattering parrots. A very large, imposing man waited next to me, leaning on his walking stick. We started exchanging pleasantries, and soon we were introducing ourselves. Philip Kulp was a retired professor of Anthropology from Pennsylvania, a Shamanic Counselor. Our conversation became very intense as the stories of anthropological discoveries in the region turned to stories of shamanism. I listened carefully to Philip explaining about shamanic journeying to other worlds to find power animals and retrieve soul parts that had left us, had been taken away, or pieces we had given away. Every aspect of my being knew the importance of this meeting, these words I was listening to ignited my soul. I asked Philip if he would guide me to my power animal. He was enthusiastic in his reply, and we made a date for my first shamanic journey just as the dogs began to bark up the road, announcing the arrival of the waylaid truck.

Bouncing from side to side, the truck backed right up to us, the storekeeper flung open the slatted doors. Two macaws flew out and into the tree, knocking over a crate of eggs that broke and dripped out of the tailgate. The dogs were licking up the yolks before being shooed away as the serious unloading began. We all examined each box as it was carried in, looking excitedly for our particular necessities for Christmas dinner.

After our feast, I encountered Philip on the beach. We had agreed to walk together for "exercize." As we greeted one another, a large white and black bird hovered, very close, above our heads. It was an Osprey, the sea eagle, blessing us. Later that evening, as darkness settled over the beach and the animals of the day quieted down, my husband and I walked through the tall reeds to the home of the shamans for our first journey to find our totem, or power animals. We lay down on some pads inside the screened porch and Philip began to instruct us about the first journey.

"Let the drum carry you. Find a hole, or entrance, into the earth. Enter, and move forward until you find your animal. Ask each animal you see 'Are you my totem animal? Are you here for my highest good?' When the drumming changes to the rapid beat of the call back, say thank you and goodbye, retrace your steps, and return to this reality."

Once the drumming began, I felt pulled and carried, into the realm of the underworld, the first journey. I emerged into the light at the entrance of a cave. Across from me sat a mountain lion, she was waiting for me. "What took you so long?" were the words that entered my being. She stood up, stretched herself, slowly, to the tip of her long tail, then gracefully leaped to my side. Two small playful babies bounded out from the cave. We played together, teasing and rolling around, until the babies fell asleep. The lion and I sat, overlooking the vista spread before us, she on my right with my hand over her back. A far off speck appeared in the distance, approaching us. An eagle, soaring gracefully, came closer and closer to land on my left shoulder. He put his head in front of my face so I cound see nothing else but the intense gold of his penetrating eye and the pure white feathers surrounding it. His right wing covered my back. I sat, comforted and protected, with my guides, until the drums called me back.

My husband told of his experience first. Nothing happened for him that he remembered. I was almost embarrassed at the fullness of my experience and cried with profound emotion while sharing my journey. The sharing seemed to further define the distance between myself and my husband. While we stayed in Costa Rica, I continued the shamanic work with Philip and his darling wife, Betty, an accomplished shamanic practioner herself. The healings were so profound that after returning to Massachusetts nothing was the same for me. I no longer was able or willing to merely exist as before. I felt trapped.

THE GREAT TRANSFORMATION

The shocking death of my godson at sixteen and my dear grandfather at 92 began a time of death for me. My uncle, aunt, and cousin passed suddenly;

the husband of my dance teacher, an active member of our community, died of a stroke the day after our last performance while we were celebrating at their home.

The last one to pass over was John, my friend, the husband of my catering partner, Sandy. Prior to the diagnosis of a brain tumor, he began to experience powerful healings with his surgical patients at the hospital. By praying with the patients, he was able to ease their minds before surgery. So many patients sent him notes of gratitude the hospital began to chastise him for his "zealotry." He was called before the Board of Directors, who ordered and threatened him to cease and desist his prayers with the patients. The Board told him to get checked out, there had to be a scientific diagnosis for his "crazy" and unacceptable behavior, for his demonstration of faith. We said our personal goodbyes. A few months later, after expressing his wish to die at home, he quietly passed, under the care of dedicated nurses who took turns, voluntarily, to come to his home and care for him, through the snow and ice of a harsh New England January, while his wife, Sandy, moved on to another lover. Each death was a reminder of the temporality of life itself. I began to ask about my own destiny. Was I destined to remain in a marriage that was hollow, lacking trust, respect or love?

Drawing on every drop of courage, I left my husband of 25 years, my friends, my community, my volunteer work, my businesses, my business partner, my home, and my dog.

In the fall of 1992, I moved to Brookline, Mass. into a small room in a friend's apartment, I was living "alone" for the first time in my life. I began my formal studies in shamanism with the Foundation for Shamanic Studies, started by Michael Harner, an anthropologist, after his own personal life-changing experiences in South America.

Way out of my comfort zone, scared and lonely, I was led to a circle of spirit guides who are always there for me, wise and kind, with the reassurance that I am never alone. Learning to trust these guides and their wisdom, trusting myself and my experiences that were not of this "ordinary" world, became my mission during this lonely time.

I found the book, "Women Who Run With the Wolves" by Clarissa Pinkola Estés, a Traditional Jungian Storyteller, to be both a challenge and a comfort. After crying my way through the introduction, the old stories and her interpretation of the mysteries, I began to understand and relate to myself in a more respectful way. I began to heal my soul wounds, and to recognize the source of my hidden anger. At this time the processes I was experiencing led to the healing steps of the Radiance Practice. With each ancient story, I remembered the ancient wounds, I began to forgive, and to let go.

RECONNECTION LEADS TO RADIANCE

Attending my first pow-wow in the summer of 1993, I met an extraordinary Native American man. Feeling a connection to each other and the Earth, we began to travel together, visiting the ancient sites nearby and learning about one another. We decided to move in together when we both found our living arrangements had to change. We found a precious home on Cape Cod in the fall. Soon, with a little cracked corn and sunflower seeds, we found ourselves the caretakers of geese, ducks and swans during one of the most brutal and snowy winters in twenty years.

We moved to Rhode Island in the spring. My Father was nearby, in a residence for the elderly and infirm, although he was neither of those. My mother had had him declared incompetent and then divorced him. I was asked to care for him by my sister, who was at that time living with my mother and divorcing her husband. This arrangement was appropriate as my dad and I were considered the "black sheep" and "crazy." We were together often. I took him out to lunch, we drove the Narragansett Trail to Newport to visit a psychiatrist every other week. The delicious lunches afterwards were, for him, the highlight of our trips. The most lovely and enjoyable times for me were when he would come up to the old homestead I had discovered at the highest hill in Rhode Island. We reconnected with the land, remembered childhood stories, and cooked comforting food at the great hearth. The family gatherings felt like a return to the ancestral home, complete with my grandmother, my children, the new puppies, and friends all around. These last years with my father brought us both a sense of peacefulness and resolve, a quiet happiness was there for all.

While I was experiencing the country life, taking care of the old homestead, and beginning to do shamanic work with a few women who had discovered me, I was asked to hold a workshop in 1995. I agreed precipitously. Realizing I had no idea what to teach, I held a Vision Quest to ask for guidance. The spirit guides and the guardians of the land gifted me with the Practice I share with you in this book. The original Practice consisted of five steps, or levels of progression. Remember, Acknowledge, Forgive, Release, and Celebrate. These steps appeared to me already written on a scroll, illustrated with picture examples of my life. One of the pictures from the future showed me teaching several students, who were really paying attention. The Workshop provided an opportunity for many of these powerful visions to come to life. At the end of the Workshop, we danced around a big bonfire to Celebrate the great Release and our Freedom. I found I loved sharing these teachings as much as learning, slowly awakening to the possibility that this may be my destiny, my work, my path.

THE EAGLE AND THE CONDOR

A massive snowstorm covered New England that January of 1996, burying us and causing severe depression for my partner. One night, the wind and snow blew the barn door open: it banged and kept me awake all night. I was hoping my partner, sleeping downstairs by the fire, would hear and get up to care for the horse. At the dawn's weak, grey light I could stand it no more. I put my boots on and waded through the snow to the barn. Crystal was covered in snow with a wild look in her eye; the inside of her stall was deep with snowdrifts, blocking the open door so it would not close. After calming her and brushing the snow from her mane, I gave her fresh food, hay and water. It took a while to shovel the snow away and close the barn door.

I felt that I was closing the door on that part of my life, too. I gathered a few clothes and left the house without saying goodbye. I was so angry that I had to go find peace for a few days. Jumping into the truck without any idea of a destination, I drove slowly north to Boston. There was a spiritual center in Cambridge called Interface, I headed there to see if there was anything of interest was being offered that weekend. John Perkins, an old teacher of mine, was giving a shamanic workshop. John, Director of the Dreamchange Coalition and author of many books, guided many seekers to the Shuar and Achuar peoples of the Amazon, the guardians of the forest. How synchronistic! I had a lot of questions for my guides. It was this workshop that provided the opportunity for me to receive a powerful vision and a prophesy that moved me from the East to the Southwest.

> *In the vision, I was an owl, flying at night. I saw a huge bonfire, with people all around. They were Elders; dressed in white with red belts, some in other native regalia. There was an entrace in the east side of the circle, where I landed, transformed into myself and entered the circle. I walked inside the circle of Elders. Facing the South, I saw a place that I knew was for me. Again, I had to walk through the fire to get to the place I knew was mine. This time, I stopped in the fire, acknowledging that it was burning all around me, yet it did not burn me. I looked at my hands; in each palm there was a flame. I acknowledged these flames in my hands with a gratefulness that nearly overwhelmed me with emotion before I took a breath, moved from the fire, walked to the place in the circle that had been saved for me, and sat down with the Elders.*

The original prophesy came from a shaman deep in the Amazonian jungle of Ecuador. She said, *The Eagle and The Condor will mate. The Feminine must come forward.* The impact of this message for me was like being struck by a bolt of lightning. I knew this message was for me! But what did it mean for me personally? Outwardly, it was clear the Eagle, a raptor, the masculine, represented North America, the Condor, a vulture, the bird that cleans the world, the feminine, represented South America. The unification of the continents and the people of the continents as partners, or mates, all walking together, was the outward prophesy.

I became more enlightened about the inner meaning of the prophesy after studying the concept of the "sacred marriage" or conjunction, put forth by Carl Jung, and later, Robert Johnson. The symbol of the "VESICA PISCES," two circles coming together to form something new, became for me, the basis of the prophesy. Relating to the ancient symbol of fertility in the Runic tradition, it also takes form as the Flower of Life, given to us by our great teacher of all, Mother Nature. The joining of the masculine and feminine creates something new, a new life, a new fertility, a new way of being.

I returned to the homestead. These messages were so profound for me that I did not talk about the vision or the prophesy, or speculate about what my part in all this may be for six months. I cherished my insights.

Then my partner, in a diabetic rage, hit me in the head, which drove me to leave. Once more, I left behind everything, the man, my home, my horse and my family. I headed West, following in the footsteps of my ancestors. I stopped in Rush, New York to stay with friends, stewards of an old tree farm, for a week. The week extended to three months as I became part of the family, feeling welcomed, safe, and loved.

Every day of that mild, beautiful spring of 1996 I walked out on the sacred land of the old tree farm in the region of the Haudenoshone, the People of the Six Nations. Lying on the ground under the giant pines, listening to the wind, I began to heal from the great insult to my sacred feminine. One day, as I was lying on the Earth crying to the ancestors, again, I asked myself the question, what can I do to heal from this place of victimhood? The answer came softly, lovingly, get up! You will find an answer at the bookstore. The bookstore? Yes, the bookstore. Placing a grateful offering of tobacco near my favorite tree, I ran down to the car and drove to town. I entered the "self help" section of the bookstore, and began to glance down the aisles for a clue as to why I was there. Suddenly, there was a finger of light that pointed to a book that was on an angle in an empty space on the bottom shelf. That was the sign I was looking for. I was taken aback by the title, "The Battered Woman" by Lenore Walker, but there was no mistaking it. This book helped me to heal myself by illuminating the abusive patterning in my life. I came to understand the pattern within me and why we allow it to continue when we do not take the responsibility to deal with and heal our anger. Every day, I asked what do I need to recognize in myself? *I was no longer a child victim, but a healthy, strong woman, able to make choices for myself.* Thanks to the peacefulness of the Tree Farm, the deer, the owl, the hawk, the snake, I felt part of the natural world, experiencing daily the cycles of life and death in this small ecosystem. Allowing myself "the luxury of time," I began to let go of the old belief systems about myself that I had unconsciously held sacred. Once these beliefs were held up to be illuminated in my conscious mind, like sheets drying in the breeze, I realized I WAS ANGRY. I recognized I was afraid of this anger, fearing it would consume me. I recalled the vision of the fire, how the flames did not burn me as I walked through the flames to the West. When I asked the Fire, the Earth, the Air, the Water, to take the anger away from me, I experienced a powerful transformation, slowly released the rage from a lifetime of mental, emotional, and finally physical, oppression. This awakening, this healing, became part of the Radiance Practice. Through this natural process of healing and listening to my guides, I was able to receive this great Blessing. I worked on forgiveness, of myself and others, every day, and I still do.

After flying from Rochester, NY, to Albuquerque, New Mexico for a gathering of the World's Indigenous Peoples, I made the decision to return to Rhode Island, rent my home, and drive to New Mexico to work with the indigenous elders who were establishing a series of gatherings in order to fulfill the prophesies of the eagle and the condor. This felt correct to me; scary, too, because what would people think? What did it matter anymore? They told me I was crazy anyway.

Further confirmation that my choice to follow the guidance was correct came from the Thunderbird, appearing in the clouds over the Mohawk Valley, as I drove next to the ancient slate cliffs, blackened with rain. The Voice I heard on the wind penetrated my very being with each thunderclap from the black clouds that drummed in waves of raindrops and maple leaves hitting the windshield. "Rise up! Rise up! The Dawn has arrived! Let all the People have Peace and be Happy!"

HEADING WEST

On the long drive to New Mexico, I found myself praying fervently, crying out to the Creator to guide me and to protect me. The fear and trepidation washed away in a river of tears as I made the long journey to the West. Moving across our vast and beautiful America, the land, the people, the ancestors, the sacred places healed me and restored my hope. The most profound sites for me were Mound City and the Serpent Mound in Ohio. It was very early in the morning that I made my visit to the city of mounds, having arrived late the night before to a small motel nearby. The Mounds are evidence of the complex societies that came before us. The full moon, setting directly to the west over the burial mound thrilled me. The astronomical perfection of the walled sacred site astonished me with its precision. The state prison across the street did not diminish the ancient power of the geometrically perfect mounds.

I sat, with my back to a gigantic sycamore tree with multicolor bark, for a few quiet moments of meditation with the ancestors. After a while, when I got up, I turned to thank the tree and bask in its beauty. There appeared before me walking sticks, praying mantis, and large bright green grasshoppers inhabiting the mottled bark. Chuckling to myself, I moved towards the Scioto River, the lifeline of the sacred center. It was still early, the museum had not opened yet. I thought I was alone. Soon, I began to see the river through the bare branches of the fall trees. Along the path were maps and drawings from Squier and Davis, two gentleman appointed by the American Ethnological Society in 1845 to compile all the information about the mounds and their contents of cultural treasure. Artifacts of copper, mica, bone and stone carvings, shells and pottery in enormous quantity were found and catalogued by Squier and Davis, in some cases these were the only record of mounds that were later plowed down, their contents crushed and broken. The giant mound that was in the center of St. Louis took three years to level amid exclamations of the great feat of earth removal accomplished in the modern way of the late 1800's. The contribution of this pair of discoverers is inestimable to the students of the Mound Cultures, and to the descendants who still live nearby, persevering in the protection of their ancestors homes and burial centers.

I sat on a strategically placed bench to dream of the canoes filled with people and goods for trade, food brought from the fields across the river, artisans creating textiles, pottery, and metalware. Suddenly, I noticed a walking stick on my right shoulder, sitting with me. She had come along for a ride to the river. She was so completely camouflaged on my shoulder, I did not see her, there she was, all the time, sitting with her hands folded, whispering in my ear the stories of the ancient times, sending me the scenes filled with the activities of the ancestors. Later, touring the museum slowly, deliciously, I opened my heart to the ancient ones, absorbing the culture I had never learned of in school.

Moving south to the Serpent Mound and another small, fine museum, I became enthralled with this unique monument to the solstices and the equinoxes, marked by the serpent with a coiled tail, head towards the river. I walked down a path that led me to the cliff under the head of the serpent, visible in the rock formation. So excited was I by my discoveries of the natural formations, I lingered a bit late after closing time and was escorted off the grounds by a frowning security guard. By dark, I had crossed to Kentucky, mostly green grass and dark brown tobacco barns on the soft hills. I turned my heart to the future, the unknown; towards new discoveries of my own? There was so much to discover through those long stretches of interstate and highways leading to the blue mountains of New Mexico, I began to view my new life with a sense of adventure.

THE EAGLE FLIES

Once arrived in my new homeland, I met often with Leon Secatero, Spiritual leader and Headman of the Canoncito Band of Navajo. We began to work together on a series of Gatherings of Elders from the North and South of the Americas. These gatherings were initiated in 1995 by Don Alejandro, The Mayan Elder of Elders from Guatemala. In fulfillment of the prophecy, which had expanded in the Southwest: "Those from the Center will Unite The Eagle of the North and Condor of the South, for we are as one, like the fingers of our hand." Don Alejandro had traveled the Americas, inviting the spiritual elders from the North and South to join him in Guatamala for the First Gathering. Leon Secatero was one of the Elders invited by Don Alejandro to represent the North. Leon was the right hand man of Don Alejandro. Together, they walked the Americas side by side, messengers of the Creator.

I BECOME DEATH

Six months later, I found myself, not in a vision this time, but in this reality, at a similar fire to the one in my vision, a Mayan Fire Ceremony in Guatemala. The ceremonial prayers, the sacred blessings, were spoken by Don Alejandro Cirilo Perez Oxlaj, Wakatel Utiw, The Wandering Wolf.

He began the ceremony with some words from the Popol Vuh, the Book of Creation of the Mayas. "Rise up! Rise up! The Dawn has arrived! Let all the people have Peace and be Happy!" Flooded with a knowing, a memory, these words filled me with an emotional confirmation that I was in the right place; I was meant to be participating in the beautiful ceremony at the sacred site of El Baul, near the birthplace of Don Alejandro and the Stela that had been erected there in his honor. Don Alejandro has recently been appointed the "Indigenous Ambassador to the World" by the President of Guatemala, one of his former students.

After the ceremony, I asked him if I could "walk" with him, to study the traditions of the people and learn the sacred prayers, the Way of the Fire. He touched my cheek gently. "We'll see," he said. At his home later in the day, he had taken my western birthday to determine my destiny according to the Mayan calendar. I was told it was my destiny to walk with him, as my day sign signified a reincarnated ancestor. Traditionally, the day on which you are born signifies your gifts, your powers, and the energies your soul is carrying or manifesting on earth. According to the Mayan tradition, your day sign is your name. My name became Julaju Keme, Eleven Death.

I was given some bright red beans, Tz'ite, to start my sacred bundle—symbol and tool of the priestess. As I walked up a steep hill from the old part of Don Alejandro's farmhouse above the river, where I was accorded my new name, I was filled with gratitude and wonder. Just then I overheard two women, students of Don Alejandro, talking about me. "Who does she think she is?" one said to the other. After my initial surprise at the judgmental tone and lack of support from the women, my fellow initiates, I realized it was a good question for me to ask myself. "Who do I think I am?" This question always brought out my ego and brought up something hurtful for me to recognize within myself. I also recognized a pattern of envy, although this was not something I wanted to admit to myself. Why would anyone be envious of me? This pattern of women betraying women, rather than supporting one another, has been part of the dominant culture since before the times of the Great Burnings. It was from that moment on that I recognized that on my walk, not only would I be before the Creator, The Fire, the Guides, my Teachers, but also before Humanity and Judgment in all its forms. My personal Radiance Practice Work began to be developed in earnest. My responses to the questions I began asking myself revealed an ancient pattern, one of many lifetimes of persecution and betrayal. This same pattern was being played out in this lifetime for me to heal through forgiveness of myself and others.

On this journey as a disciple, a humble student, so much ancient wisdom was to be learned. It seemed as if a whirlwind had accelerated my life experiences. For the next two years, walking with the Elders, practicing the ceremonies, learning the different dimensional levels of the Fire ceremony, I began to experience life each day through the awareness of the energies of the day signs of the Sacred Tzol'kin Calendar. My DNA began to shift and awaken. I began to trust the experiences that the Cosmos was providing and revealing to me each day as my life unfolded. Through the instruction of the thirteen ceremonies at the Sacred Sites in Guatemala, and turning my problems over to the Creator, I began to surrender to the energy of the Cosmos rather than trying to "control" everything or to "do something". When I did not feel in alignment, I began to ask questions: "What is the purpose? Do I want to put my energy here?"

These questions brought a new perspective, a knowing. My new way of being did not come easily. I was sorely tested. Saying no was not in my previous conditioning. Rather, I wanted to please others, to give generously in the hope that everyone would like me, and I often misplaced my trust in others, giving away my power. Because of my pattern of codependency, along with believing men were better/wiser/smarter than women, and that women needed men, it took many years to shift my patterns of conditioning. As the powers of discernment developed in me, the Radiance Practice work was tempered and refined.

INITIATION

In 1998, I was initiated as a priestess, or, aj'ik, a "Ray of Light," in the Mayan tradition. The ceremony took place at the home of Don Alejandro in Totonicapan in the highlands of Guatemala. Fragrant, freshly gathered pine needles were strewn on the terrace. The altar was overflowing with flowers, scented and colorful, surrounding the ancient altar stones and the images of the beloved Maximon. I was one of six students who shared three fires in comales, shallow dishes of clay.

My fellow initiates and I wore crowns of flowers. We had made them the night before with great festivity. The musicians, engaged by Don Alejandro, were present for dancing on the eve of graduation, as well as for the initiation feast. The morning of our ceremony, it began to rain. Tin roofing was put over the altar and our three fires. The rain on the roof added a natural musical blessing to the day. The fires blazed and talked, spiraling up, as they told us about the future of our sacred paths.

Each of us was called forward to receive our blessing from the Ancestors. Don Alejandro placed his hand on each of our heads and his other hand on the largest of the sacred stones to transmit the message from the Ancestors

SUZANNE ELIEL

SUZANNE ELIEL

across space and time. After receiving our personal transmission and blessing, we welcomed the elders, priests, and priestesses from the region. Then, we danced, celebrating our initiation! Our two-piece band played into the night until they fell over with fatigue and drink.

The next day, we had a large ceremonial fire for the day of 7 T'zi, the last day of the old year on the 260-day sacred calendar. A bit more somber that morning, we released all that had occurred over the past year in this ceremony. Don Alejandro called the children, our hope for the future, to the inner circle for a blessing. We were charged with protecting the children. The fire burned so hot it made a permanent scorch mark on the terrace of Don Alejandro's home.

The following day, "Wajxakib Batz," we welcomed in the New Year. All of the graduates, our band, and the family of Don Alejandro traveled to the nearby ancient sacred site, with its nine altars on a mountain cliff overlooking a beautiful river valley. Down below us a mighty waterfall thundered. The great stones were black with smoke from the millennia of ceremonies.

SUZANNE ELIEL

We wore our crowns of flowers and carried our crosses and sacred bundles to be easily recognized as initiates in front of those in attendance at the New Year's Fire. We prayed for what we wanted for the New Year, for ourselves, and for the whole world. We read the fire and its predictions for the quality of the coming year. Many New Year's Fire celebrants acknowledged us as graduates, with our crowns of flowers, as being part of the thousands of traditional people who had come to celebrate the New Year.

SUZANNE ELIEL

HEALING THE MIND

In 1999, soon after my initiation, I began hypnotherapy studies in California at the Alchemical Institute of Hypnotherapy, led by David Quigley, an extraordinary Merlin of our times. During these studies, I felt much like the young Arthur in the presence of a powerful Druid Teacher. There was a confirmation and connection with my spirit guides and ancestors that was strengthened and bonded in the deep healing that occurred within me during this intense, deep, and personal program. Forgiveness of self, myself, was the work. The techniques used were shamanic in nature, with the same powerful results—transformation of habits, habitual thinking, abuses, and vices.

When our mind is in alignment with our spiritual path, our destiny, we are able to retrain ourselves, retool and recalibrate our old ways of thinking. What occurs in our brain is that our neurons actually move into an alignment, much like telephone wire, where everything is bundled together. A myelin sheath forms around the bundle to protect it and keep it in alignment. Every time we practice, our brain returns to the bundle of the memory of this practice, and our body responds. The same bundling process occurs regardless whether we are playing tennis, riding a bike, or practicing a more disciplined way of thinking. There is scientific truth to the saying "practice makes perfect."

The Radiance Practice was deeply reinforced and strengthened with visualization techniques learned during this training, culminating in my Certification as a Master Hypnotherapist.

THE CELTIC CONNECTION

Leon Secatero and I had been invited to Ireland along with several other Native American elders to a gathering at Darver Castle hosted by Margaret Connolly, the Ban Fasa ne Eire, the Wise Woman of the Land. After our presentations and a tour of some of the greenest sacred sites in the world, Newgrange, Knowth, and Tara, the Hill of Kings, we drove north to Armagh where we, as Americans, presented Margaret with a Belt representing the Unification of the People. The presentation ceremony took place at the sacred mound of Macha. Subsequently, a unification and peace has occurred in Ireland.

We all flew to England to honor the sacred sites of Stonehenge, Avebury, and Silbury Hill. We were permitted to enter the circle of stones at Stonehenge at 6:00 am, before the monument opened to the public. We were blessed to be there at sunrise, when Leon sang a ceremonial song to call back the Spirit of the Horse. It is the Spirit of the Horse that will carry us into the next 500 years. Leon always asked, "What will we carry with us into the next 500 years?"

THE SODIZIN CEREMONY

When we returned from our amazing and sacred time in the land of the Celts, Leon and I were asked by a Navajo Elder to produce a documentary about a sacred ceremony, a ceremony that had not been performed in over 170 years. The Navajo Elder, medicine man, and former Code Talker, Grandfather Martin Martinez, requested that we document the ceremony to preserve the traditional knowledge for future generations. The documentary was filmed on Mount Taylor, in New Mexico, one of the four sacred mountains of the Navajo People. After producing the "Sodizin Ceremony, the Reunion of Mother Earth with Her Children," I was invited to show the documentary in various locations across America, as well as in Ireland.

Others asked me to teach about the Mayan Calendar and to interpret individual horoscopes in the Mayan way; or to do divinations by reading the sacred tzi'te beans in my sacred bundle, part of my training as a priestess. Working at this deeper level with the energies of the days, I began to recognize the influence of the days on the consciousness of my clients and myself. Powerful healings, profound answers and solutions occurred for those who requested personal readings. The readings bring forth the knowledge of who we really are and serve as a catalyst for movement from whatever repetitive patterns or "stuckness" that may cause us to feel trapped. The horoscopes illuminate our path, our lives, and our destiny. The steps of the Radiance Practice naturally came forward as a way to forgiveness and detached compassion, a way to healing.

I ASK THE QUESTION

In mid-winter of 2006, I was early for an appointment in the North Valley of Albuquerque. It was dark in the valley next to the Rio Grande, as I waited by an abandoned field in front of an old adobe home. Rich and fertile, river valleys stimulate the fertility of the mind. Valleys have always been "home to the priestesses." It was a new moon, and so dark; I had a sensation of being out of time. As I waited, trying to keep warm in the chill of the night, I asked the question, "Is it time to write about this Practice?"

The answer came so quickly; I struggled to sit up from my semi-recline, reached for my notebook and turned on the light. Barely able to write fast enough, the word "Radiance" came, and with it, three more steps to complete the practice.

There is no time to waste. It is time to ask. Get over the ego and get on with the healing! Ask the Self, for all wisdom is within. Experience has given us each wisdom. Time now, to awaken your wisdom and re-create yourself, your life. Create new boundaries for yourself. Move into a place of honesty, without shame or judgment; tempered with compassion and sensitivity. Trust in the practice and trust in yourself to be reborn into radiance.

This message is for everyone.

PART II

GUIDE TO THE
MAYAN CALENDAR

THE MAYAN CALENDAR

Upon hearing about where we are now in the context of Time according to the Mayan Calendar, many would ask the question, "What can we do?" The simple answer is: prepare. These current Times have been given many names: The Return of the Ancestors, The Return of The Knowledge, The Return of the White Buffalo Calf Woman, the End Times, and many more names from different cultures and calendars from around the world. What does this mean to us? Our indomitable spirits know something is "going on" on a bigger scale. We recognize things; the weather, for example, is changing. The Calendar confirms these changes are real for us and gives us the knowing. As we begin to receive, we recognize the return of the Knowledge.

Within the Mayan calendar, we have come to the end of a period known as the "Nine Hells." Many hundreds of thousands of us remember the summer of the "Harmonic Convergence." A period of five hundred years came to an end in August of 1987.

Sit back and remember that year—1987—was it a transformational time for you? Whenever we come to the end of an era, or the end of anything, there is always a new beginning. The "Harmonic Convergence" of August, 1987, also marked the beginning of the era known as the Thirteen Heavens, our Bridge to carry us over 2012, The Year Zero, and through the End Times.

The Thirteen Heavens, by its name alone, is a beneficial period for humans. The clouds of confusion and dark energies that have been over the Earth are dissolving; we can begin to reconnect with Father Sky, we can reconnect with the Light, the Radiance from the Heavens. Grounding ourselves on our Earth Mother, we become intermediaries of Light, transmitters of love and light to our Earth Mother. We can choose to be Radiant, and create Light over the Earth. This is the message of the calendars in the time of the Thirteen Heavens.

One way to become enlightened and fully participate in the time of the Thirteen Heavens is to receive the gift of the Radiance Practice. Radiance is our natural state of being, a part of the innate human essence. The shining, glowing expressions of love and joy that we see in the smiles and actions of our children and grandchildren are also a part of us. As we grow up, this innocent way of being can fade, as we absorb belief systems and the old ways that belonged to a different, wounded, generation.

Now, at this time, we are being asked, and given the opportunity, to heal the woundedness of ourselves and our society. We are all connected by our thoughts and feelings through the collective unconscious. One energetic thought of hope, love, gratitude, or forgiveness enters the collective and filters through the network of thoughts, connecting us all, giving us all the power of hope, love, gratitude and forgiveness.

One of the beliefs that has been passed on to us in our society is the belief that we can change others. This is a false belief system whose time has run out. The truth is, we have all the abilities we need to change ourselves, and our way of thinking about ourselves. We are not responsible for "changing" nor are we able, to change another. The opportunity for self empowerment is present, here and now, for everyone. Take it! Take it for yourself! Become responsible for your personal healing.

As we heal, becoming Radiant, we will attract others who are also Radiant. At the same time we may experience others who do not want us to be our Radiant selves. Here is where we must draw on our tools of self-reliance, the powers we all have but that are probably dusty from disuse! Discernment is a key tool to dust off now. Discernment is our intuition, our ability to comprehend, without Judgment, then making an informed choice with our free will. Discernment is insight, a powerful tool for recognizing old belief systems and old relationship patterns. The choice of how we act is the gift of our free will. Move the Judge and Ego aside, become impartial, and observe all the opportunities equally. Why not? There is much to be gained from choosing the correct path.

All of us who are alive here and now are here for a reason. The calendar day on which we were born tells our destiny and purpose. It shows us our strengths, and our particular gifts. It offers the tools we may need, where we may make mistakes, what pitfalls may occur, and what particular challenges and obstacles we may face as we "walk" the sacred path of our lives, our destiny.

Over the years since my initiation and subsequent teaching, I have become a day keeper, or "keeper of days" of the calendar round known as the Tzolkin, the 260-day sacred calendar. The cycles of Life, our beloved Earth, the

Cosmos and the Universe are in my awareness as each new day begins with a greeting to
the Sun and the energies of the day. As a day
keeper, I begin and end the day with a prayer
to the Creator, a prayer of gratitude and alignment which serves to amplify my awareness
of the energies of the day. I am always grateful
for what I receive.

*The choice of how
we act is the gift
of our free will.*

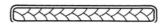

The Mayan calendar anchors us to the Earth, to the Cosmos and to all
Living Beings. There are 20 days and 13 numbers that rotate together like the
gears of a clock to form the sacred calendar: the Tzolkin. This is the calendar
of 260 days or nine months—the gestation period of a human being.

MAYAN CALENDAR
Long Count

August 11
3114 B.C.

December 21
2012

- Approximately 5,200 years equals one Period of the Sun

- August 1987: end of the Time of the Nine Hells and the beginning of the Time known as the 13 Heavens

- 1987–2012 is known as "The End Times," The Return of the Ancestors, The Return of the Knowledge

- All other calendars are within and part of the Long Count calendar.

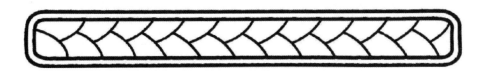

THE DAY SIGNS

B'ATZ
bahtz

E'E
aay

AJ
aaak (guttural)

IX
eesh

TZ'KIN
z kin

AJMAC
ak mak

NO'J
noch (guttural)

TIJAX
tea hash

CAWOK
cawook

AJPU
ak pooh

THE DAY SIGNS

IMOX
emosh

IK'
eek

AK'AB'AL
ak ah ball

K'AT
kaat

KAN
kaan

KEME
kemay

KIEJ
keeech (guttural)

Q'ANIL
kan eel

TOJ
toch (guttural)

TZ'I
zee

SYNCHRONICITIES OF THE CALENDAR

one day = one Kin

The Wayeb' is the Five day Calendar

20 days = one month, hun Winak

260 days = Tzolkin, the Sacred Year

360 days = one Tun

7,200 days or 20 years = one K'atun

144,000 days or 400 years = one B'aqtun

Every 52 years The New Fire Ceremony marks the alignment of the Sun and the Pleiades, from the Galactic Center, through the Earth.

Every 52 years, the 260 day sacred calendar and the 360 + 5 day calendars conjunct.

13 B'aqtuns equal one Period of the Sun, 5,200 years, ending Dec. 21, 2012

Five of these B'aqtun cycles equals a precessional cycle of 25,627 years, ending Dec. 21, 2012 when the Solstice Sun will be "reborn" from the Galactic Center.

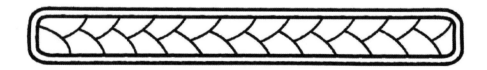

December 21, the Winter Solstice, has always been associated with Winter, Night, and the Rebirth of the Sun after a period of darkness. The ancient sites of Newgrange, Nowth, and Dowth in Ireland and Stonehenge in England, constructed at the beginning of this solar cycle, were aligned so the winter solstice sun would penetrate a dark tunnel, ignite a symbol of rebirth, eternal life, on the wall, the triskik, then light a "fire" beneath a stone bowl containing the bones of the Ancestors, symbolizing the return of the light, the knowledge, the ancestral energy, the rebirth of hope to our world.

When viewing the Milky Way, one can see the "dark rift" in the path of stars known to the Mayas as the "Sak Be" the White Road, the road of our Ancestors. The ancient glyphs depict this place in the Milky Way as the place of the Rebirth of the Sun, with the Sun god being born from the mouth, or "the dark rift" of an alligator, the primordial being. This "dark rift" is also known as the Womb, or Place of Birth, with the stars of the Milky Way as the milk of the Galactic Mother, ready to nurture the New Sun, the New World, the Rebirth of the Divine Wisdom, the Rebirth of the Consciousness of Love.

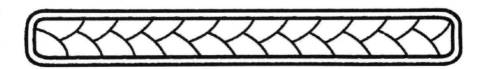

VENUS CYCLE; VENUS REAPPEARS AS THE MORNING STAR
EVERY 584 DAYS

VENUS TRACES A FIVE POINT STAR AROUND THE ELLIPTIC
EVERY EIGHT YEARS

Q'ANIL
THE SEED
THE PLANET VENUS

One of the great mysteries of the Maya world is the story of Quetzalcoatl. Was he man whose stories of the time when he walked the earth have come down to us in Myth? The ecliptic is the pathway in the sky around which the stars of the Zodiac revolve. Where the Milky Way and the Zodiac cross is the Galactic Center; between the Zodiac signs of Sagittarius and Scorpio, at the foot of Ophiucus. Ophiucus, "the man with the serpent," is the 13th constellation. "The Serpent Bearer" relates to Asclepious, the Greek Healer, son of Apollo, the Sun. The healing energies of the "man with the serpent" can also relate to Quetzalcoatl, for in the Nahuatl language, the quetzal is the sacred bird with long, green tail feathers that undulate when flying; coatl means snake. The name Quetzalcoatl is the "Feathered Serpent."

Quetzalcoatl was always associated with the virtues of enlightenment and spiritual purity, love, compassion, respect and reverence for all living things; he was a teacher of justice, science, agriculture and the arts, especially metal working. He was a teacher of writing and rituals marking birth; he was the Bringer of the Calendar. Revered by the people as a Holy Man, Quetzalcoatl was opposed to the practice of human sacrifice. His enemies devised a way to humiliate Quetzalcoatl through treachery and betrayal, forcing him to suffer, driving him away. As Quetzlcoatl left to the direction of the East, he instructed the people to LOVE ONE ANOTHER.

He promised to return, to be reborn. The period of the Nine Hells is over, we are all experiencing the beginning of something new, The Thirteen Heavens. The Light is available to us once again after a long period of darkness. All the energies from the Cosmos and the Universe will pass through this healing place, the Thirteenth constellation, the Galactic Center, in 2012. It has already begun, enabling and preparing us for this Transformation, our Rebirth into the new period of the Sun.

PART III

THE STEPS TO RADIANCE

ANCIENT SANSKRIT PRAYER

Creator, You who are the source of all power,

and whose rays illuminate the whole earth,

illuminate also my heart,

so that it may do your work.

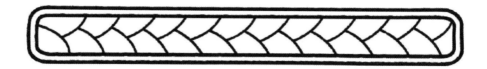

NOJ
KNOWLEDGE AND WISDOM
FROM THE EARTH, COSMOS, UNIVERSE:
THE KNOWING

RECOGNIZE

When we want to change something, an aspect of ourselves for example, the universe will provide a situation for us to recognize, in order for us to bring it to our conscious mind. This puts us in a state of recognition, or the feeling that we have met this before. We can choose to admit that this thing we are recognizing is something that we already know. We realize, or make real, the existence of the thing that is now present in our conscious mind.

Often, without recognizing it, we are given Knowledge. We receive this knowledge in different ways: from Nature, our Guides, asking a question, school, books, television, movies, different life experiences. We gain lots of knowledge, but it doesn't mean we are automatically wise. When we begin to experience and take responsibility for our lives using our knowledge—what we already know—that is when we move into the realm of wisdom, the state of being wise. Wisdom is knowing about ourselves, about the way things are, without illusion. Experiences that provide knowledge and wisdom are lights on our soul's path. They help awaken our soul memory and guide us to return to the sacred wisdom we carry within. We learned it here, on Earth, in this third dimensional school, in past lifetimes. When we repress or deny our wisdom, we become estranged from the very source of our own power.

Reincarnation is a part of the day sign Keme, death, after which the cycle continues with Rebirth, the mystery and awesomeness of Life. When we pray before the Fire on the day of Keme, we cry out, "Please don't let us die an unrepentant death!" We are asking to have the wisdom to turn away from our old ways and to dedicate our lives to amending our path. We are always given the opportunity to discern our lessons in this lifetime, to continue with our forward progress and to enhance the growth of our souls. Earth is the school for us, where our souls learn their lessons of this lifetime. Like a pioneer classroom, with children of different ages and levels of learning, our souls are studying different lessons in this lifetime with individualized lesson plans.

When we are children, we are a cup of innocence waiting to be filled. Most often, our cups are filled with belief systems and old ways of being that no longer serve us when we grow up, becoming adults. We are like sponges, absorbing old beliefs, for they help us survive when we are small. Old beliefs become a part of us, so ingrained in how we act, talk, and function on this planet that they are no longer separate from us. These old beliefs also decay in our unconscious, dimming our Radiance and disallowing our souls to learn the lessons needed to gain wisdom. As adults, our guides will bring up these old beliefs to our conscious mind and make them manifest with the help of our emotions, especially anger, sadness, fear, panic, and frustration.

We often respond to the beginning of this process with denial. Now, in these times, we must allow the remembering. Our subconscious will not release any information to our conscious mind that we cannot handle. Our guides take good care to protect us. At the same time, they provide for us the opportunity to grow by doing the "work."

Sometimes, we do not allow these rememberings because we fear our emotions and their perceived power over us. Emotions are often the "trigger" that project us into a place of recognition. When we are so angry at the same old, same old, or S.O.S., it is a cry for help. When we experience our own S.O.S, we can propel ourselves to take action by asking the question:

What is it in me that needs to be recognized and healed?

You will be presented with an image, an awakening, a knowing. Allow yourself to remember, to bring forward this knowing, and give it form.

AJMAC
RADIANT, SPIRITUAL COMMUNICATION
AND COMMUNION WITH THE GUIDES
IN A STATE OF FORGIVENESS:
ILLUMINATION OF MIND

ACKNOWLEDGE

Once we have recognized an old belief system, we must acknowledge and accept it, own it. It is ours. Whatever the issue, such as not being "nice," we have carried it a long way. We can be grateful, too, for it has helped us to get this far! You are not a child any longer and you have survived. You are in charge.

We may feel remorse, dread, sadness, guilt or fear associated with this old system. These are lower forms of energy that we are able to illuminate and transform immediately by moving into the state of Forgiveness. The emotions we feel are related to the old way of thinking and being with the issue that has arisen. Breathe yourself into calmness as you realize the "panic fear" is only an old feeling. Move gently into a peace of mind. Recognize your strength. When the acceptance of our past experience takes place, there often is a release of energy that is healing for us. From this detached, compassionate forgiveness of self, forgiveness of others, ALL healing can occur. To do this, we must fill ourselves with Love for ourselves. This may bring up an internal struggle; we are being asked to shift from our unconscious patterns of thinking and talking to ourselves in the old way.

WHY CAN'T YOU BE NICE?

About 1980, at Easter, the children were making Little Mermaid Easter eggs at my mother's home in Rhode Island. I can recall the beautiful, watery iridescence of the eggs as they emerged from the swirling surface of the dyed water.

Suddenly, my husband questioned me in a frustrated and angry way, "Why can't you be nice?" Something about this question made me immediately bristle. My sense of awareness was alerted, standing ready. Everything came forward and I knew "nice" was not right for me. Not even addressing the "why can't you be ..." part of the question, I responded to the word "nice."

I said, "I'm not nice. I don't like that word."

My husband responded, "Well, if you're not nice, what then?"

We were sitting in a triangle, my mother to my left, my husband to my right. I said, "Let's think of another word besides nice" and at that moment, the word POWER appeared behind my eyeballs, in FLAMES! The vision of power and flames was really close, so there could be no mistake. Taking a deep breath,

I said, "How about powerful?"

They both leaned forward, palms facing me: moving their palms back and forth for emphasis, they responded simultaneously, "No, no, no. You don't want to be powerful!"

Shocked by their reaction to the idea of me being powerful, I backed down, and said, "Okay, how about strong, or kind?" This seemed to be acceptable to both of them; they sat back. The danger was over for them: I had not realized my own power.

Webster's Collegiate Dictionary lists the first meaning of the word "nice", from the Old French, as: foolish and wanton, ignorant: ignorant and not wanting to know.

"Aha!" I finally understood. Surprised and amused, I also recognized that my "not wanting to know" was actually a form of denial. For all those years, was I not recognizing my own denial? Such denial had hurt many generations who had come before me. Descending from the Proper Victorian Era Family with its circumspect upbringing style, we had a tendency, or a rule, to ignore and not speak of certain things that were perceived to be damaging to the reputation of the family. I can remember phrases like, "Don't wash your dirty laundry in public." In other words, don't talk about anything that could possibly be wrong with the family, such as depression, suicide or mental illness. It was all about what other people would think, as if there was a perception of weakness when any emotion was displayed. For my family, we put on the mask of "I'm Fine" in public.

When my therapist suggested I might be depressed, my reaction was denial. Not in my family! However, when the symptoms of depression were explained to me, I had to acknowledge I felt a new awareness and an awakening from a vast state of denial. I recognized the pattern of depression in my family and I acknowledged the depression in me as I moved though a "masked" depression into a full blown "clinical" depression. It was the ideal place to begin transformation.

CONDITIONAL WORDS

I can/I can't/I should: indicating someone trying to hold power over us, most often ourselves, judging ourselves and others by our old belief systems. We are giving away our power. These words take away our power.

Change to

I will, I will not: Consciously choosing and using these words, we take our power back. We stand in our own power and are able to exercise our free will from our own strong center.

Shifting into love and support for ourselves is a difficult task, requiring us to change our continual internal chatter. This chatter, the talk we talk to ourselves, is affecting every cell of our being. Along the path, we have taken over the voices of others and made them our own. We are being shown these thought patterns to bring them to our conscious mind. We have heard and assimilated negative put downs, attitudes of blame of self and others. We are keeping our own selves down, hiding our own radiant light under a pile of the old SOS. Now, it is time to let go of all recrimination of self and others.

Accept that a shift has begun to new pathways of thinking and speaking to ourselves with LOVE.

K'AT
GRAVITATIONAL FORCE,
MAGNETIC ATTRACTION, THE NET,
THE STATE OF BEING TRAPPED

DISCERN

Does it still serve me?

When we recognize and acknowledge what we are bringing forth to heal, we have given it form, separated it, and chosen to work on it. We have forgiven ourselves. We then are able to ask the question,

"Does it still serve me?"

With this question, we are asking our mental body, our physical body, our spiritual selves, and our emotional body. With this question, we are going to get a direct answer from our higher self and our guides. All are working in concert to help us. When we recognize that something no longer serves us, then what do we do with it? To heal it and allow it to leave you, simply wrap it in your love.

THE BAD TEACHER

At the final consultation at a teacher's college, the counseling professor tells the senior student, "You will never succeed as a teacher." Forty years later, the student, upon putting in her retirement request from a microchip development company, is told, "Please do not retire! We want you to teach the incoming trainees because you are the most knowledgeable and patient. The accuracy of your work has guided our entire company to achieve amazing success in our highly competitive and technical field."

Forty years is a long time, almost a lifetime, of believing something that is not your Truth.

AJ'PU
THE SUN, THE WARRIOR,
THE HUNTER, THE ANCESTORS

INITIATE

With the Radiance Practice, we are beginning something new, a new journey for healing. We are going down a path in our brain that we have not taken before. We prepare for this as we would a road trip, or a flight, gathering what we need for the journey.

Dust off your courage, you will find it in your heart. Courage lives in all of us: It is an important part of our Radiance, waiting to be called upon when needed. We aren't able to see our own courage often when we are children, because our fear is small. We need bigger fears to activate courage. For me, the paralyzing fear was that I would never realize my true self, my truth, my destiny. What is your fear? Where do you feel your courage? Call it out!

In this part of the visualization, you will need to imagine something sharp, like a sword, or a knife. This will be your tool to "cut away" that which no longer serves you. I always seem to be in a flowing, white goddess dress with a very shiny and very big sword ... the appropriate gear will appear to you. You will know.

These tools will appear to you in "the etheric plane," an imaginary dimension close to our reality. What we activate in the etheric plane now will manifest in our physical reality very quickly, as Time has accelerated; there is an urgency in us to "get it done."

TIJAX
THE KNIFE,
FREEDOM,
HEALING

ACTIVATE

In this part of the visualization, we are going to take action to free ourselves from the "trap" of our old way of thinking. As we turn our focus to inward healing, visualization becomes one of the important tools we can choose for our healing. The action we take in the "etheric plane" has an immediate effect on us, spiritually, physically, and emotionally. When we commit to this action of cutting away, we are taking back our power. We acknowledge the resurgence of our courage and our warrior-ness. Our natural, instinctual behavior is freed, our instinct for survival, the instinct to protect our Honor and stand in our Truth. The healings that occur in the etheric plane will be reinforced by our changed ways of thinking and talking to ourselves in this reality. In this step, we will use our tool of the sword: do you need armor? A shield?

A very important part of this step is taking care of your energy, the energy that has been attached to the other for so long. After you have cut away the form of the part of yourself that no longer serves you, Watch and Feel your own energy returning to you first. Then, watch the form drift away, in its cloud of love, and disappear on the horizon. This will lead us to the next part of the visualization, where we naturalize and welcome the return of a part of ourselves, our own energy.

KAN
THE SERPENT,
THE SPIRAL OF OUR DNA,
THE GALAXY, EVOLUTION

NATURALIZE

By cutting away that which no longer serves us, when our own energy returns to us, we feel a sparkling, or "body lightning" in our spinal column, in our DNA, and in every cell in our bodies. We are assimilating and reuniting with our own energy. It is important to stay within this state of reception and reunion, letting it happen.

You will know when to continue when you feel a calmness, a settling down, like a pond, after a stone thrown into the smooth surface, returns to the former state. It looks the same, but there is something new in there under the glassy surface. Recognize the healing that has occurred. We have healed and freed a form of the ancestral debt, or karma, that we have carried for so long. We have cut it away for our descendants. We are not going to carry that which no longer serves us into the Future. By healing yourself, you are healing the world.

B'ATZ
THE THREAD OF TIME,
THE UMBILICAL CORD, SPIRITUALITY,
THE POLES OF MASCULINE AND FEMININE

CELEBRATE

Celebration is honoring a time of joy, a commemoration of giving thanks. We are grateful to our guides and ourselves, no one else did this for us: we have done it for ourselves. We acknowledge our inner strength, we acknowledge our power, our gifts. We are honoring and celebrating who we are. We are not perfect, we are spiritual, loving, radiant beings and it is time to Dance!

When we cut away a part of ourselves, there is an empty space. The universe does not like emptiness and will fill the space, most likely with something that does not belong to us. The most important part of this practice is to bring back to ourselves that which we have been looking for, that which we have been missing in our lives.

We want to fill ourselves with the higher vibrations of Love. Dancing, singing, music, and laughter express the higher vibrations of love and have been a part of celebration for thousands of years! We have missed dancing with abandon, singing love back into ourselves and into our Mother Earth. When we are dancing, the vibration of our feet sends love, healing love, into the Earth. The bottoms of our feet connect to and awaken the Earth. When we dance, we become intermediaries of LOVE between Heaven and Earth.

How do you imagine the Dance? The bonfire leaping into the air as you dance to an insistent drum? A solemn processional dance before a solstice ceremony? The solo dance on the beach as the Sun glitters on the sea and the

50

sand? The community dance with our partners, circling, spiraling, shouting out in honor of the Harvest?

Dancing our animal, animating our power animal, in trance, brings forward our true selves, whole, alive, and connected to All That Is.

When I dance to "Night Fever" by the Bee Gees (yes ... Disco), I am smiling! The smile is a powerful tool and an extraordinary gift that sparkles and radiates through our bodies. Feel good, and the smile radiates outward from ourselves just like a mirrored disco ball. The Radiance bounces back to us when we dance, sing, celebrate. We become like that—radiant and reflective of the joy and light within.

Laughter is a part of celebration! Let's get over our own "seriousity" and lighten up! Fill up with light and love, become your radiant self. Move, shake and shimmy, moving your hips especially, bringing forward the feminine abundance of ourselves. Feel the gratitude and appreciation for your body, a gift for this lifetime, your temple of Love.

CAWOK
HOUSE, FAMILY, COMMUNITY,
THE SUSTENANCE OF THE WORLD

ENJOY

To enjoy life once again, we must move into a place of simplicity, or simple enjoyment. When life becomes so complex and busy, we lose parts of ourselves to all the distractions and chaos that is placed in our path to divert us from our life's journey, our soul purpose.

Consider your path. Slow down. Breathe deeply, this is your LIFE. There is JOY in everything! There is BEAUTY all around us. Honor it. Feel it. Experience it.

Commit to Life, to Living your Life in Radiance.

WAYS TO SIMPLIFY

Be grateful

Be generous

Be respectful of all life

Behave like the elegant being you are

Stop watching the News

Stop watching TV commercials

Stop reading the daily newspaper

Do not gossip; Praise! Find the good in everything

*Do not swear—when you find these words coming from you—
  Bless it, instead of cursing it*

*Ask yourself the question, "Do I need this?"—before any
  purchase, before eating anything*

Eliminate clutter: one drawer, one closet, one room at a time

Talk to the birds, animals and trees, reconnect with Nature

Acknowledge, gratefully, the source of your nourishment

Ask for help or solutions from your guides—always and often

Encourage the children of the future generations

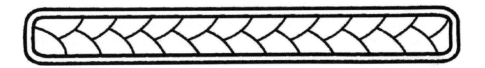

KEME
REBIRTH

THE FUTURE IS NOW

We have developed a tendency, due to our conditioning, and a belief that we "need to know everything," to "lock on" to the old forms, and the negativity of life over the past 500 years of the Nine Hells. 1987 moved us into the Thirteen Heavens and a time of new focus and comprehension, an awakening. Raise your sights, set new goals for yourself. then focus on the steps toward what you want.

Manifestation will occur faster now, in these times of the Thirteen Heavens. Stay focused on the positive, lighten up your outlook. Move into a way of being that is in conscious alignment with the future you are envisioning for yourself and the world.

We are in a time of great, unlimited potential for humanity. How we relate to ourselves, to one another, is based on our desire for transformation; we make it happen. When we are experiencing our lives on a higher vibrational level than we have in the past, when we have taken the responsibility to manifest our own potential through the use of our free will, we gain a new perspective of great wisdom.

Certain words, frequencies, and vibrations awaken our DNA. When we relate to ourselves with more Respect, with more Love, when we feel and speak to ourselves and others with LOVE, we become able to overcome obstacles, including the desecrations to our environment, doing what we must, together, to preserve, perpetuate, and continue the forward movement.

Presently, we live in a world that seems hostile and dangerous, downright scary, a world that makes fun of spirituality, kindness, of softness, yielding, peacefulness or relaxation. When we are wound up so tightly, when we are rigid, judgmental and stubborn, we break. By bringing forward Forgiveness, Tolerance, and HOPE, we can build new foundations that are built on the higher frequencies of Community, Cooperation, and Compassion.

This work of bringing back Spirituality to ourselves, our families, our communities, is a WORK that extends far beyond this present time, it will never be lost, for we carry it in our souls as RADIANCE.

May your Blessings be Bountiful!

PART IV

THE RADIANCE PRACTICE
WORKBOOK PAGES

NOJ
KNOWLEDGE AND WISDOM
FROM THE EARTH, COSMOS, UNIVERSE:
THE KNOWING

RECOGNIZE

Sit quietly. Call forth your guides, asking for help and guidance. Say the ancient prayer, preferably out loud. Breathe deeply. Recall a time when you became angry, hurt or upset. When you have in your mind the recollection of the incident with all the accompanying feelings, ask yourself the question:

What is it in me that needs to be recognized and healed?

The answer will come, breathe . . . and be patient with yourself. When the answer comes—a picture, some strong words from an argument, a strong feeling, be with it, knowing you are safely observing the incident and all the players, including yourself, from a new perspective. Give what you recognize a form to work with for this visualization.

Write it down in the Workbook.

AJMAC
RADIANT, SPIRITUAL COMMUNICATION
AND COMMUNION WITH THE GUIDES
IN A STATE OF FORGIVENESS:
ILLUMINATION OF MIND

ACKNOWLEDGE

Fill yourself with Love for yourself. Allow the Light of Love to illuminate your mind, radiating Love and Light outwards in all directions. At the same time, feel the warmth of the Light penetrating your mind, melting away the lower forms of energy with the Spirit of Forgiveness. From this place of Illumination, know that all healing will occur with the forgiveness of self; the forgiveness of others. You are in communion with the guides and you feel their Love for you. As you are expressing your Love for them, they are sending you their love in waves, as the waves of the ocean rise up on the shore, they also return to the Source with your Love. Ask the Creator to forgive you unconditionally, and you forgive the Creator.

Write your experience in the Workbook

K'AT
GRAVITATIONAL FORCE,
MAGNETIC ATTRACTION, THE NET,
THE STATE OF BEING TRAPPED

DISCERN

Does it still serve me?

Discern what is not your truth and prepare to release it. Visualize what you recognize in a form that you can release; such as an imaginary "nice" or "unsuccessful" aspect of yourself. Wrap it in your Love AND PREPARE TO LET IT GO.

Visualize the form in front of you, and all that has been illuminated with your Love.

When you are ready, ask the question; Does this still serve me?

Write the answer in your Workbook.

AJ'PU
THE SUN, THE WARRIOR,
THE HUNTER, THE ANCESTORS

INITIATE

Practically, be comfortable, quiet, with no distractions, and have what you will physically need close by, like tissues, a glass of water, your workbook, and a candle if you wish.

Breathing deeply and slowly; ask your guides and your ancestors for protection and guidance, for the highest good of yourself and all living beings.

Summon your courage. What is your fear? Where do you feel your courage? Call it out!

Imagine something sharp, like a sword, or a knife. This will be your tool to "cut away" that which no longer serves you. The appropriate gear will appear to you. You will know.

These tools will appear to you in "the etheric plane."

TIJAX
THE KNIFE,
FREEDOM,
HEALING

ACTIVATE

Breathing deeply and slowly, visualize yourself in the etheric plane. You may recognize this place from your childhood. It may be a beach, a forest glade, or vast nothingness. You are dressed. Notice the details of your clothing. Feel the sword in your hand. You are standing in your power. See and Feel your Radiance. Look down, and see a cord of attachment coming from your solar plexus, just beneath your ribs. This cord may appear delicate but strong, like a spider's thread, or as large as a great ship's rope. Looking to the other end, you see the form you have given to the old belief about yourself. Place a cloud of Love around the form and around yourself. Often, the cloud of Love will have beautiful, iridescent colors. When you feel ready, focus on the cord of attachment. Lift your sword high and cut the cord. Use your Strength! Use your Will and your Courage!

Watch the energetic cord of attachment return to you. You are receiving back your own energy that has been attached to the other for so long! Feel it return to you, breathing deeply, continue to receive your energy until the cord is no longer visible. Then, still breathing deeply, watch the other form drift away in the cloud of Love. It drifts far away to the horizon, until it disappears.

KAN
THE SERPENT,
THE SPIRAL OF OUR DNA,
THE GALAXY, EVOLUTION

NATURALIZE

Breathe. Keep breathing, being present with your self. You have freed yourself and become more real. As your energy realigns and reactivates within you, you feel a sparkling or "body lightning" in your spine, in your DNA, in every cell of your body. Keep breathing and stay with this healing as long as necessary. Feel the vitality returning and recharging you. Keep breathing, feel the communion and communication, feel the gratitude and love from, and for, your guides.

Allow yourself to fully receive this blessing.

B'ATZ
THE THREAD OF TIME,
THE UMBILICAL CORD, SPIRITUALITY,
THE POLES OF MASCULINE AND FEMININE

CELEBRATE

Feeling good, smile at yourself. You begin to hear the soul music that activates you and propels you into the dance. Celebrate, and fill yourself with Love, Love for yourself and all living things. Dance with abandon!

Slowly, when you are ready, come back to this reality. Say a big "thank you" to your Guides. You will bring the energy of Love for yourself, the Joy of the Dance within you, as you return to this reality. You will remember everything, especially the healing, as you bring your Light, your Power and your Radiance within you, back to this reality.

Continue breathing deeply until you feel fully present. As you become fully present, open your eyes.

Write your experiences in the Workbook.

CAWOK
HOUSE, FAMILY, COMMUNITY,
THE SUSTENANCE OF THE WORLD

ENJOY

Consider your path. Slow down. Breathe deeply, this is your LIFE. There is JOY in everything! There is BEAUTY all around us. Honor it. Feel it. Experience it.

Commit to Life, to Living your Life in Radiance.

Write your new awareness of what, where, when you find yourself in a state of enjoyment in the workbook.

Every day, when the Sun rises and creates the opportunity for a new beginning, acknowledge it. Say the ancient prayer, feeling the sun's rays penetrating you, penetrating your heart, and radiating outwards from you, to the World.

This is your ongoing homework.

ANCIENT SANSKRIT PRAYER

Creator, You who are the source of all power,

and whose rays illuminate the whole earth,

illuminate also my heart,

so that it may do your work.

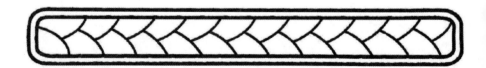

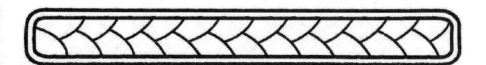

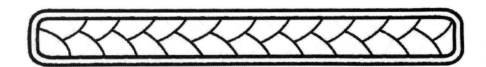

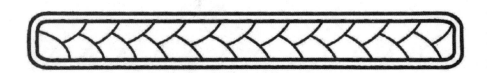

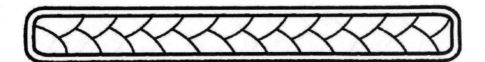

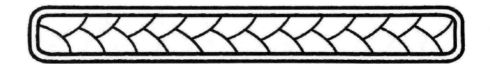

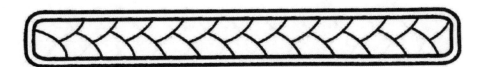

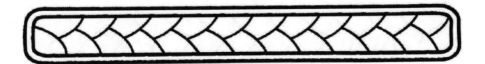

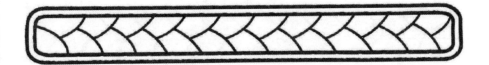

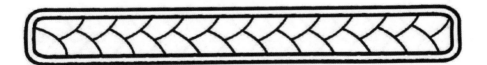

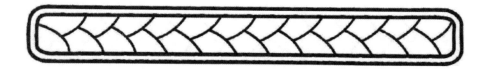

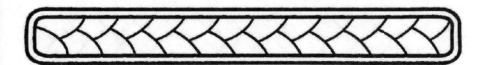

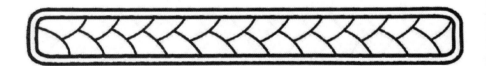

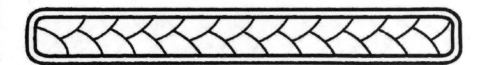

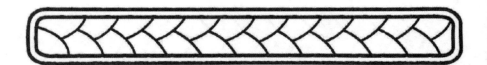

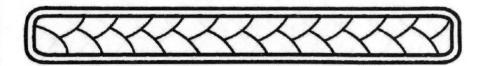

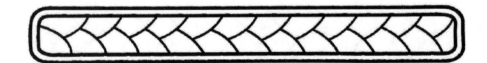

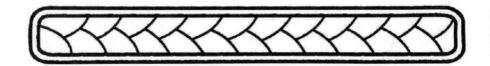

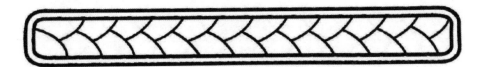

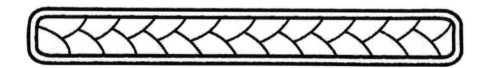

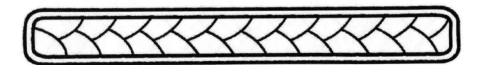

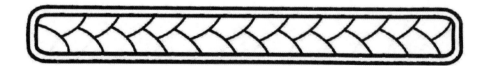

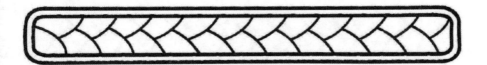

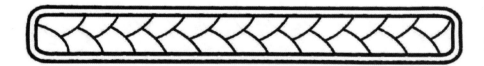

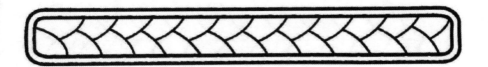

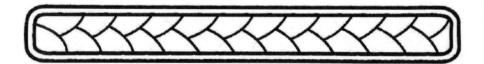

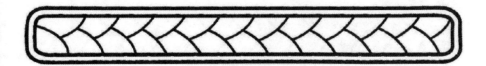

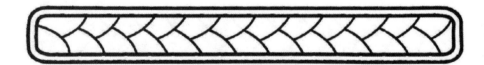

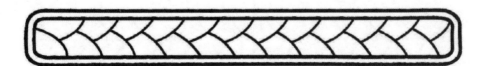

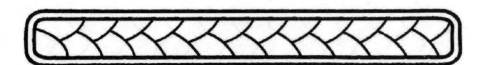

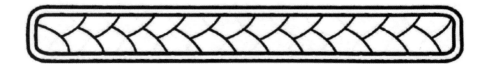

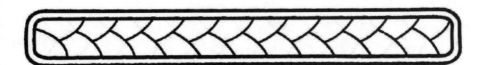

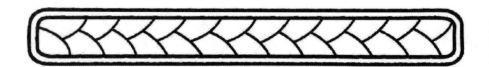

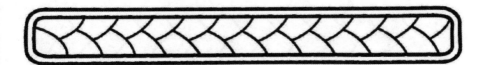

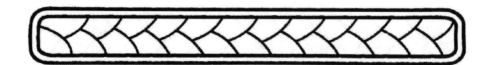

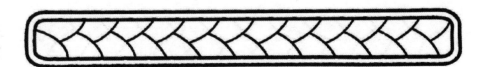

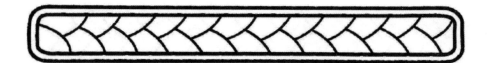

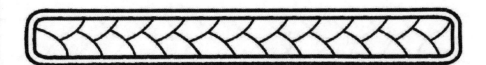

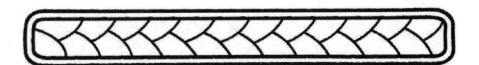

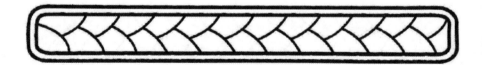

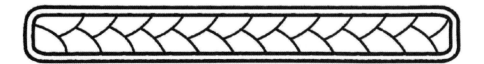

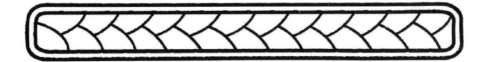

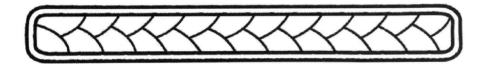

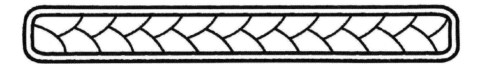

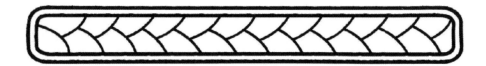

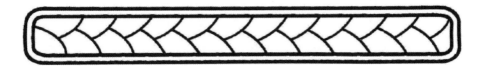

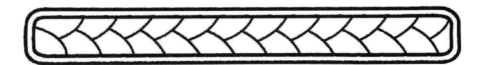

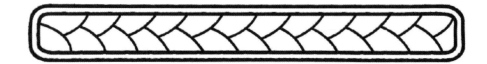

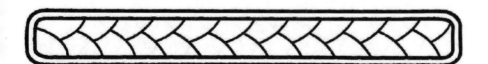

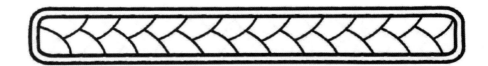

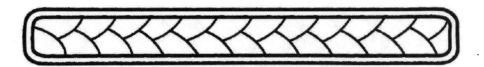

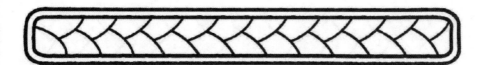

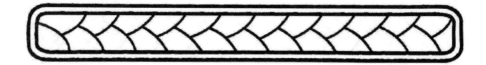

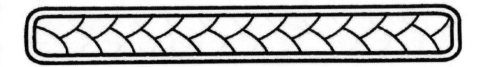

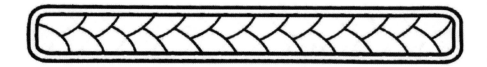

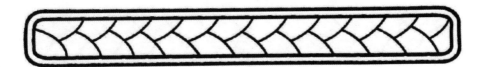

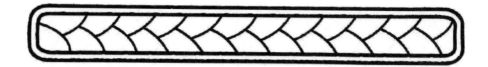

BIBLIOGRAPHY

Webster's Ninth New Collegiate Dictionary. Merriam-Webster, Inc., Springfield, Mass. USA, 1990

Popol Vuh. translated by Dennis Tedlock, Touchstone, Simon and Schuster, 1985, 1996

Time and the Highland Maya, Revised Edition. Barbara Tedlock, University of New Mexico Press, Albuquerque, New Mexico, 1982

Maya Cosmos, 3000 years on the Shaman's Path. Linda Schele, David Freidel, Joy Parker, William Morrow and Company, Inc. New York, New York, 1993

Galactic Alignment. John Major Jenkins, Bear and Company, Rochester, Vermont

Astrology, Karma, and Transformation. Steven Arroyo, CRCS Publications, P.O. Box 1460, Sebastopol, California, 95472, 1978, 1992

Mythic Astrology. Guttman & Johnson, Llewellen Publications, St. Paul, Minn., 1993

Imagery in Healing, Shamanism in Modern Medicine. Jeanne Achterberg, Shambala, Boston / London, 1985

Soul Retrieval: Mending the Fragmented Self. Sandra Ingerman, HarperCollins, New York, New York, 1991

Jaguar Wisdom, Revised Edition, Kenneth Johnson, Archive Press & Communications, *www.archivepress.com*, 2009

KEME
DEATH,
REINCARNATION,
REBIRTH

ACKNOWLEDGMENTS

This workbook is dedicated to my ancestors, parents, siblings, children and grandchildren—what wonderful teachers you are!—for the healing of the ancestral traumas, and the healing of the generations to come.

All of the experiences, perceptions, and mistakes are mine. However, there are certain messages in the Radiance Practice that seem to be of a global, cosmic, or universal nature. My gratitude is flowing, like the waves of the sea, to the Source, for sending these messages.

There is no harm intended in this Workbook, only joy, and love for life and the lessons life has taught me. I hope to be a student for a long time; there is much work to do.

My gratitude is boundless for my friends: Darlene, whose encouragement got me started; Karen, who knows how to ask the questions; and Rachel, without whose help, guidance, support, and healing this workbook would not have come to fruition.

Angela Werneke, Cosmic Artist, how touched I am when I look at the cover of this book! Along with Karen Stroker, book composer and literary midwife, you have manifested my vision of The Radiance Practice Workbook. Thank you, Jennifer Esperanza, for capturing the Radiance.

Thank you to Don Alejandro, the Wandering Wolf, who took me into the pack and led the way. Thank you to Don Ruffino, for his kindness. Thank you to Judy Annamaria Perez and Don Pedro Cruz, my godparents, who, along with the comadres and compadres, baptized me in the mountains above Lake Atitlan. Thank you to the Elders who included me in the studies of the Codices at the edge of the sacred Lake Atitlan.

Thank you to the World, the Sacred Places, and the Guardians of the Sacred Places.

Cynthia was born in Hawai'i and dedicated to the Goddess Pele at six months. In 1997, she died, and was reborn. She began to study Shamanism at the Foundation for Shamanic Studies in 1992. In 1996. she moved to New Mexico to begin work on the Gatherings of the Elders of the North and South in fulfillment of the prophesies of the Eagle and the Condor. In 1998, she was initiated as a priestess in the Mayan Tradition by Don Alejandro Cirilio Oxlaj at his home in Guatemala. 2001 brought the cofounding, with Leon Secatero, of Friends of the Indigenous Elders, a non-profit organization. Under the auspices of Friends, she produced a video documentary, *The Sodizin Ceremony, The Reunion of Mother Earth with Her Children.* She is the author of *Freeing the Light Within, The RADIANCE Practice Workbook.*

Cynthia is available for Mayan Horoscopes, Divinations, and Workshops on the Mayan Calendar & The RADIANCE Practice.

DIVINATIONS
Do you have a question?
Life Path, Love, Money, Work
Relationships
Ask the GUARDIANS OF THE DAYS OF THE SACRED MAYAN CALENDAR

MAYAN HOROSCOPES
The Mayan Calendar Day Signs carry all the energies of The Earth,
The Heavens The Cosmos and the Universe.
What energies are you manifesting ?
What energy is carrying you?
Call 505-867-8087 to make an appointment with your Destiny

www.freeingthelightwithin.com
www.theradiancepractice.com

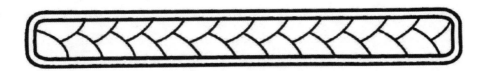